To Tigger
G.A.

For my Mom and Dad
D.W.

First published in the United States 1997 by
Little Tiger Press, 12221 West Feerick Street,
Wauwatosa, WI 53222-2117
Originally published in Great Britain 1996 by
Orchard Books, London
Text © 1996 Giles Andreae
Illustrations © 1996 David Wojtowycz

Library of Congress Cataloging-in-Publication Data
Andreae, Giles, 1966-
Rumble in the jungle / Giles Andreae ; illustrated by David
Wojtowycz.
p.   cm.
Summary : A poetic exploration of the hippos, leopards,
chimpanzees, and other animals found in the jungle.
ISBN 1-888444-08-8
1. Jungle animals—Juvenile poetry. 2. Children's poetry, English.
[1. Jungle animals—Poetry. 2. English poetry.]
I. Wojtowycz, David, ill. II. Title.
PR6051.N4R86 1997 821'.914—dc20 96-34423 CIP AC
Printed in Hong Kong / China
First American Edition
5 7 9 10 8 6

Rumble in the Jungle

Giles Andreae

Illustrated by
David Wojtowycz

Little Tiger
Press

There's a rumble in the jungle,
There's a whisper in the trees,
The animals are waking up
And rustling the leaves.

The hippo's at the water hole,
The leopard's in his lair,
The chimpanzees are chattering
And swinging everywhere.

Some animals are frightening,
And some are sweet and kind,
So let's go to the jungle now
And see who we can find . . .

munch   munch

Chimpanzee

It's great to be a chimpanzee
Swinging through the trees,

And if we can't find nuts to eat
We munch each other's fleas!

Lion

The lion's the king of the jungle,
Who quietly sits on his paws.
But everyone quivers
And shudders and shivers
As soon as he opens his jaws.

Elephant

It's great to be an elephant
All big and fat and round,
And wander through the jungle
Just elephing around.

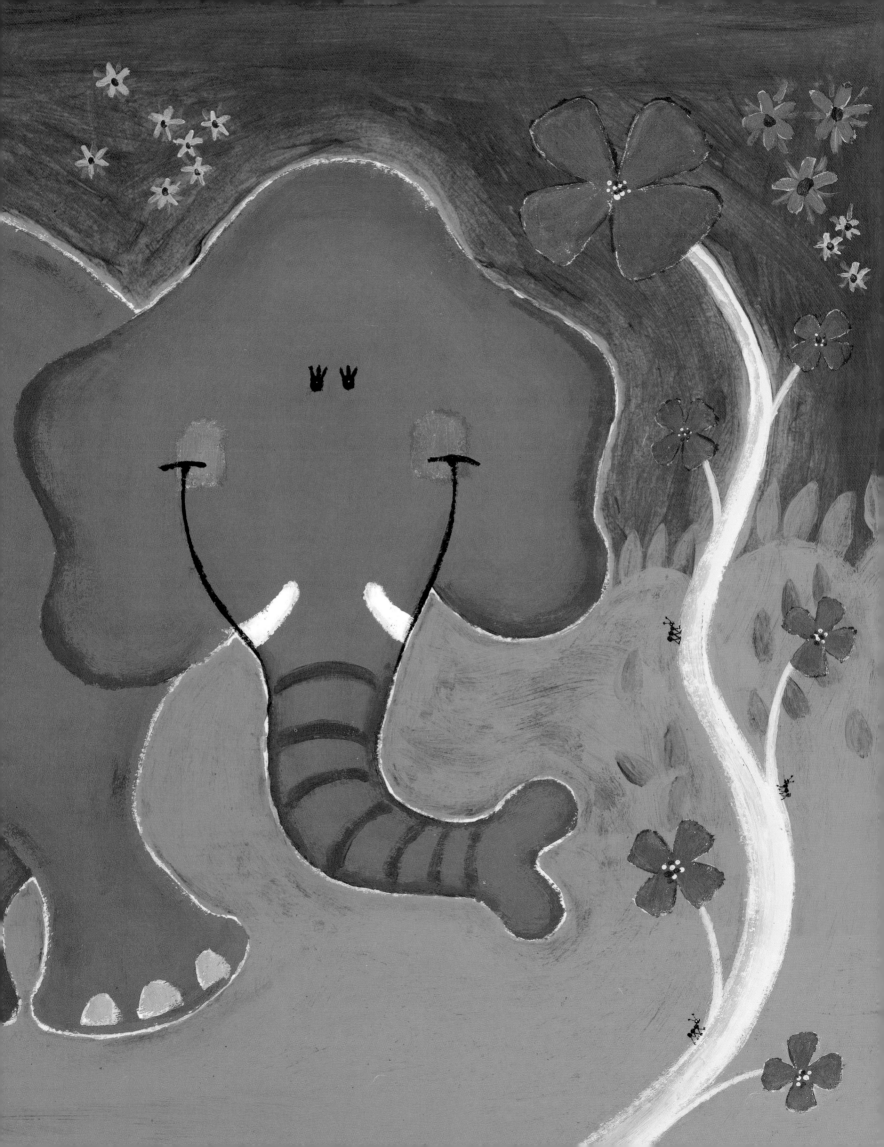

Zebra

I could have been gray like a donkey
Or brown like my cousin the mule,
But instead I've got stripes,
Which my ladyfriend likes,
Since they make me look handsome and cool.

Snake

The boa constrictor's a slippery snake
Who squashes then swallows his prey.
He knows that it's not very friendly or kind,
But they do taste much nicer that way.

Ssss

Giraffe

Some animals laugh
At the gangly giraffe
But I hold my head up and feel proud.
I really don't care
When my head's in the air
And my cheek's getting kissed by a cloud.

Hippopotamus

Hello, I'm a big happy hippo,
I sleep in the sun till I'm hot,
And when I'm not sleeping
I mooch in the mud,
Which hippos like doing a lot.

Crocodile

When animals come to the river to drink
I watch for a minute or two.
It's such a delight
To behold such a sight
That I can't resist chomping a few.

Rhinoceros

The ravenous rhino
Is big, strong, and tough,
But his skin is all baggy and flappy,
Which means that there's plenty
Of room for his lunch,
And that makes him terribly happy.

Gazelle

No one can run half as quickly as me,
The galloping, gorgeous gazelle.
I can leap up so high
That my horns touch the sky,
And I'm awfully pretty as well.

Gorilla

The gorilla is big, black, and hairy,
And the thing that he likes to do best
Is to look all ferocious and scary
And wallop his giant great chest.

Leopard

If you meet a hungry leopard
Prowling through the night,
Make sure you call him *sir*
And be incredibly polite.

Tiger

Beware of the terrible tiger,
You don't always know when he's near,
But his eyes shine like lights
In the blackest of nights,
And his growl makes you tremble with fear.

Grrr

The night has started falling
But the jungle never sleeps,
The vultures circle slowly
While the leopard softly creeps.

And if you listen quietly
You might just hear the growl
Of a hungry pair of panthers
Who are still out on the prowl.

The lions and their little cubs
Are sleeping in their den,
So let's leave them till tomorrow
When we'll visit them again.